Phonics Tales! ™

gr

A Groundhog Named Grady

by Teddy Slater
illustrated by Tammie Lyon

SCHOLASTIC INC.

New York • Toronto • London • Auckland • Syd
Mexico City • New Delhi • Hong Kong • Buenos

Designed by Maria Lilja
ISBN-13: 978-0-439-88469-3 • ISBN-10: 0-439-88469-1
Copyright © 2006 by Scholastic Inc.
All rights reserved. Printed in the U.S.A.

First printing, December 2006

12 11 10 9 8 7 6 5 4   7 8 9 10 11/0

Grady was a little **groundhog.** He lived with his family in a **great** big hole in the **ground**.

Grady had a mom, a dad, a **grandma**, and a **grandpa**. He also had a big brother named **Grover** and a big sister named **Grace**.

They all thought **Grady** was the **greatest** little **groundhog** in the world. Except for one thing. . . .

Grady was a **grabber**! **Grady grabbed** all the **grapes** out of **Grandma's** fruit bowl.

Grady grabbed Grace's green balloon.

And **Grady** was always **grabbing Grover's** toy **grizzly** bear.

Once **Grady** even **grabbed Grandpa's** whiskers.
"Ouch!" **Grandpa groaned**.

"**Grady**," **Grandpa grumbled**, "would you please stop **grabbing** everything!"
But **Grady** just **grinned**. Then he **grabbed Grandma's** glasses.

One day, **Grady's** whole family went for a **group** walk in **Greenwood Grove**.

A **great** big rosebush was **growing** by a **gravel** path. **Grady** reached out to **grab** a flower. "Be careful!" **Grandma** warned.

But it was too late. **Grady grabbed** the
thorny stem.
"OUCH!" **Grady groaned**.

"Poor **Grady**!" cried **Grace**, **Grover**, Mom,
Dad, **Grandma**, and **Grandpa** all together.
No one said, "That's what you get for **grabbing**."
They didn't have to.

From then on, **Grady** never **grabbed** anything again. Well, hardly ever!

GR Riddles

Listen to the riddles. Then match each riddle with the right *gr* word from the box.

Word Box

grow   grasshopper   grapes   Grace   green
gray   groundhog   grandma   grin   grass

1 There will be six more weeks of winter if this animal sees its shadow.

2 Peas are this color.

3 This fruit comes in bunches.

4 This is another word for *smile*.

5 This girl's name rhymes with *place*.

6 This grows all over the ground.

7 Little Red Riding Hood went to visit her.

8 When you water a plant, it does this.

9 You get this color when you mix black and white paint.

10 This green insect likes to jump.

GR Cheer

Hooray for *g-r*, the best sound around!

Let's holler *g-r* words all over town!

There's **green** and **grab** and **grass** and **grandma**.

There's **grow** and **group** and **grapes** and **grandpa**.

There's **grouch** and **gray** and more words still—

Like **groan** and **greet** and **gross** and **grill**.

G-r, g-r, give a **great** cheer,

For the **grandest** sound you ever will hear!

Make a list of other *gr* words. Then use them in your cheer.